For Jaclyn, my favorite songwriter, and her Jasper — S. S.
To Rachel and Matthew — D. S.
For Charlie and Leo — M. C.

Barefoot Books
294 Banbury Road
Oxford, OX27ED

Barefoot Books
2067 Massachusetts Ave
Cambridge, MA 02140

Text adaptation copyright © 2014 by Sunny Scribens
Illustrations copyright © 2014 by David Sim
The moral rights of Sunny Scribens and
David Sim have been asserted

Graphic design by Judy Linard, London
Reproduction by B&P International, Hong Kong
Printed in China on 100% acid-free paper
This book was typeset in D K Mama Bear,
Fiddleshticks, Futura and Nightclub
The illustrations were prepared in gouache,
acrylics and pastels

Lead and backing vocals by Mark Collins
Musical arrangements © 2014 by Mark Collins
Flutes and saxophones by Brad Grant
Drums performed and recorded by Tim Weller
Piano, organ, bass, strings and guitar by Mark Collins
Recorded, mixed and mastered by Clive Cherry
at Tongue and Groove Studios, London
With thanks to Zoë Blackford and
Gareth Owen Sound for the great sound effects,
and to the children's ensemble from Julie Sianne Theatre Arts:
Olivia Bowden, Maddie Fairbank, Jade Marner,
Samantha Osborne and Natasha Tait

Animation by Thomas Barth, Sophie
Marsh and Sarita McNeil

Hardback with enhanced CD ISBN 978-1-78285-097-7
Paperback with enhanced CD
ISBN 978-1-78285-098-4

British Cataloguing-in-Publication Data:
a catalogue record for this book is available
from the British Library

Library of Congress Cataloging-in-Publication Data
is available under LCCN: 2013051236

1 3 5 7 9 8 6 4 2

Barefoot Books would like to
thank astronomer and science educator
Dr Carie Cardamone, PhD (Astronomy),
for her invaluable help in reviewing the
scientific accuracy of the book, and
writing the thrilling endnotes.

SPACE SONG ROCKET RIDE

Written by Sunny Scribens
Illustrated by David Sim
Sung by Mark Collins

Barefoot Books
step inside a story

In the universe spins a galaxy. It's a spiral of stars called the Milky Way.

10 9 8 7 6 5 4 3

1 BLAST OFF!

And the bright stars shine
all around,
And the bright stars shine
all around,
And the bright stars shine all around.

In among the stars
of that galaxy
Is our solar system
where eight planets spin.

The planets that spin
in the solar system
in the galaxy

Where the bright stars shine

all around,

all around,

Where the bright stars shine all around.

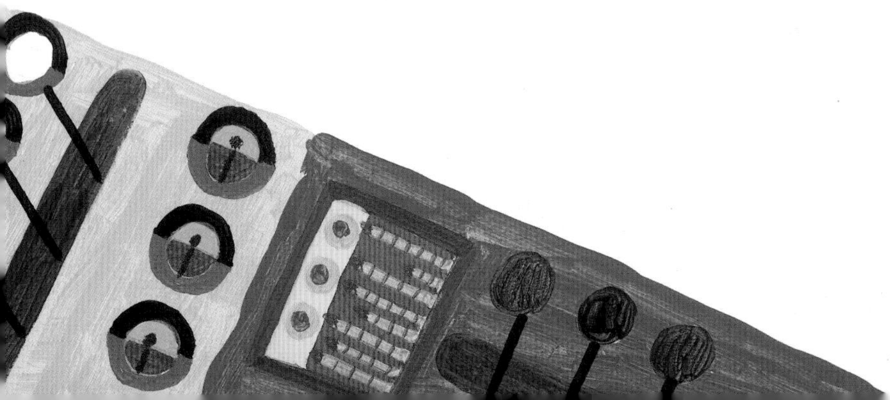

In the middle of the planets shines a burning sun.

The sun's our own star — a bright, blazing ball.

The sun in the middle
of the planets that spin
in the solar system
in the galaxy

Where the bright stars shine all around, all around, all around,
Where the bright stars shine all around.

And around that sun
orbits our blue earth
Blue from the water
that gives us life.

The earth around the sun
and the sun in the middle
of the planets that spin
in the solar system
in the galaxy

Where the bright stars shine all around, all around, all around.

Where the bright stars shine all around.

And around that earth
orbits a moon,
Turning every month,
tugging at the tides.

The moon around the earth
and the earth around the sun
and the sun in the middle
of the planets that spin
in the solar system
in the galaxy

Where the bright stars shine
all around, all around,

Where the bright stars shine all around.

Down on the earth
we watch the sky.
The twinkling stars
wink down at us.

The stars in our eyes
and the moon around the earth
and the earth around the sun
and the sun in the middle
of the planets that spin
in the solar system
in the galaxy

Where the bright stars shine
all around,
all around,
Where the bright stars shine all around.

The Universe and Us

We live on planet Earth. Seen from space it looks blue because it is mostly covered in water. Earth is just one of eight planets in our solar system. The sun that you see rising each morning and setting each evening is at the middle of our solar system. It is orbited by four rocky planets — Mercury, Venus, Earth and Mars — and four giant gas planets: Jupiter, Saturn, Uranus and Neptune.

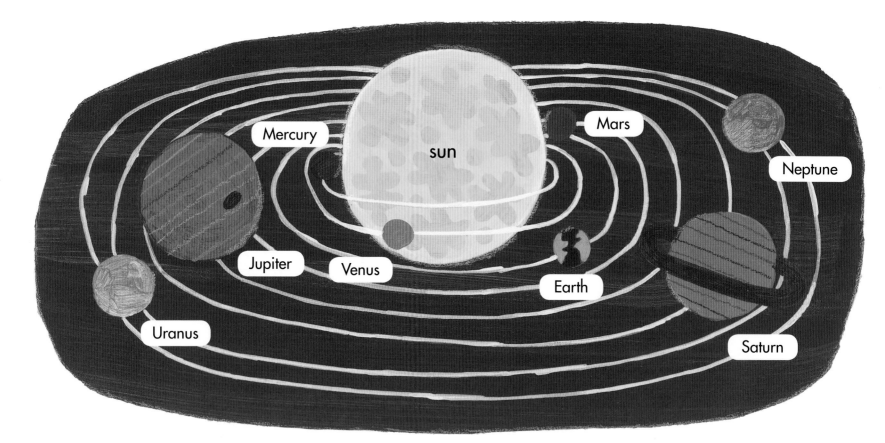

Our sun is a star — a burning ball of gas. It is one of many billions of stars in our galaxy, which is called the Milky Way. Each of the many stars in the night sky is a sun like our own, and many of them have planets orbiting them. Our galaxy is just one of many billions in the universe, each of which contains even more stars and planets than there are grains of sand in a sandbox.

Amazing Things in the Universe

Moons are usually rocky objects that orbit planets. Just as the earth orbits the sun once each year, our own moon orbits the earth once each month. Other planets have moons too — Jupiter has over fifty!

Satellites are man-made machines that orbit the earth and other planets. They collect data and transmit phone and TV signals. Some can be the size of a truck! Old satellites are abandoned in space — they become space junk.

Shooting stars are small asteroids, called meteors, which burn up in a planet's atmosphere. You can see them as beautiful streaks of light that shoot across the sky.

Asteroids are rocky objects that are much smaller than planets. They range from the size of a house to the size of a whole city.

Black holes are powered by gravity, the force that keeps your feet on the ground. They appear to be black because the gravity is so strong that not even light can escape once inside. Unlike stars they don't shine, so you can't see them directly!

An Astronaut's Life on the International Space Station (ISS)

Two hundred miles up above the earth, astronauts are living on the International Space Station. It is continually orbiting the earth. The astronauts float around rather than walk, because there is no gravity. They sleep in sleeping bags attached to the wall with velcro, so they don't float away while they sleep! The ISS was planned and built by scientists and engineers working in fifteen different countries.

Eating: Most food on board comes in packets and may need water added to it before eating. But astronauts do eat fresh fruit and vegetables! Liquid is drunk through a straw from a carton because otherwise the droplets would float around.

Playing: Astronauts enjoy many of the same activities you do here on Earth: they watch TV and movies, play music, read books, sing, sew and can call or e-mail family and friends. They also have to exercise each day.

Going outside: Astronauts sometimes go on space walks. This could be to do experiments, test new equipment or repair satellites or spacecraft. A special space suit protects them from the harsh environment of space and provides them with oxygen to breathe.

Space Song Rocket Ride

The Future of Space Exploration

Humans explore space using robotic spacecraft commanded from Earth, such as this one, called Voyager. It left Earth over thirty years ago and is now venturing farther into space than ever before. It has recently reached the outer edges of our solar system!

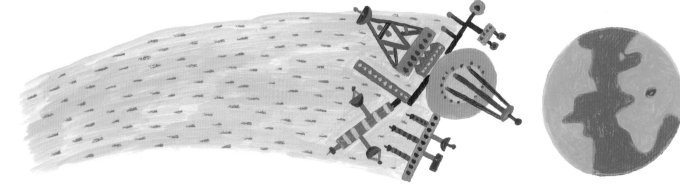

Space exploration is changing fast. What do you think space robots will look like twenty years from now? And what might they find?

Barefoot Books
Step inside a story

At Barefoot Books, we celebrate art and story that opens the hearts and minds of children from all walks of life, focusing on themes that encourage independence of spirit, enthusiasm for learning and respect for the world's diversity. The welfare of our children is dependent on the welfare of the planet, so we source paper from sustainably managed forests and constantly strive to reduce our environmental impact. Playful, beautiful and created to last a lifetime, our products combine the best of the present with the best of the past to educate our children as the caretakers of tomorrow.

www.barefootbooks.com